I0486666

Monthly Planner

Feel free to tweet about, blog about,
and tell your friends about
The Journal Box

Thank you!

WWW.THE JOURNALBOX.COM
sales@thejournalbox.com | 215-298-9475
The Journal Box: Woman, Minority, Veteran Owned Company.
@2021 - The Journal Box

ISBN 978-1-4357-6523-8

The way to get started
is to quit talking
and begin doing.
Walt Disney

MONTHLY PLANNER

MONTH:

MONDAY	TUESDAY	WEDNESDAY	THURSDAY	FRIDAY	SATURDAY	SUNDAY

NOTES

PRIORITY

DAILY PLANNER

MOOD: 😊 🙂 😐 🙁 😢

WEATHER:

APPOINTMENTS

07:00 AM
08:00 AM
09:00 AM
10:00 AM
11:00 AM
12:00 PM
01:00 PM
02:00 PM
03:00 PM
04:00 PM
05:00 PM
06:00 PM
07:00 PM
08:00 PM
09:00 PM

NOTES

WATER INTAKE TOTAL:

DAILY PLANNER

DATE:

MO | TU | WE
TH | FR
SA | SU

MOOD:

WEATHER:

APPOINTMENTS	NOTES
07:00 AM	
08:00 AM	
09:00 AM	
10:00 AM	
11:00 AM	
12:00 PM	
01:00 PM	
02:00 PM	
03:00 PM	
04:00 PM	
05:00 PM	
06:00 PM	
07:00 PM	
08:00 PM	
09:00 PM	

WATER INTAKE TOTAL:

DAILY PLANNER

DATE:

MO | TU | WE
TH | FR
SA | SU

MOOD:

WEATHER:

APPOINTMENTS

07:00 AM

08:00 AM

09:00 AM

10:00 AM

11:00 AM

12:00 PM

01:00 PM

02:00 PM

03:00 PM

04:00 PM

05:00 PM

06:00 PM

07:00 PM

08:00 PM

09:00 PM

NOTES

WATER INTAKE TOTAL:

DAILY PLANNER

MOOD:

DATE:

MO | TU | WE
TH | FR
SA | SU

WEATHER:

APPOINTMENTS

07:00 AM

08:00 AM

09:00 AM

10:00 AM

11:00 AM

12:00 PM

01:00 PM

02:00 PM

03:00 PM

04:00 PM

05:00 PM

06:00 PM

07:00 PM

08:00 PM

09:00 PM

NOTES

WATER INTAKE TOTAL:

DAILY PLANNER

DATE: | MO | TU | WE
| TH | FR
| SA | SU

MOOD: 😊 ☺ ☺ ☹ 😢

WEATHER: ☀ ⛅ ☁ 🌦 🌧 ❄

APPOINTMENTS

07:00 AM

08:00 AM

09:00 AM

10:00 AM

11:00 AM

12:00 PM

01:00 PM

02:00 PM

03:00 PM

04:00 PM

05:00 PM

06:00 PM

07:00 PM

08:00 PM

09:00 PM

NOTES

WATER INTAKE TOTAL:

5

DAILY PLANNER

DATE: | MO | TU | WE |
| TH | FR |

MOOD: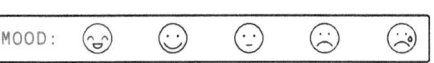

WEATHER: | SA | SU |

APPOINTMENTS	NOTES
07:00 AM	
08:00 AM	
09:00 AM	
10:00 AM	
11:00 AM	
12:00 PM	
01:00 PM	
02:00 PM	
03:00 PM	
04:00 PM	
05:00 PM	
06:00 PM	
07:00 PM	
08:00 PM	
09:00 PM	

WATER INTAKE TOTAL:

DAILY PLANNER

DATE: MO TU WE TH FR SA SU

MOOD: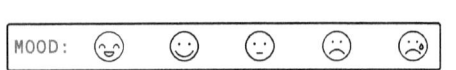

WEATHER:

APPOINTMENTS	NOTES
07:00 AM	
08:00 AM	
09:00 AM	
10:00 AM	
11:00 AM	
12:00 PM	
01:00 PM	
02:00 PM	
03:00 PM	
04:00 PM	
05:00 PM	
06:00 PM	
07:00 PM	
08:00 PM	
09:00 PM	

WATER INTAKE TOTAL:

DAILY PLANNER

MOOD: 😊 🙂 😐 🙁 😣

WEATHER:

APPOINTMENTS	NOTES
07:00 AM	
08:00 AM	
09:00 AM	
10:00 AM	
11:00 AM	
12:00 PM	
01:00 PM	
02:00 PM	
03:00 PM	
04:00 PM	
05:00 PM	
06:00 PM	
07:00 PM	
08:00 PM	
09:00 PM	

WATER INTAKE TOTAL:

DAILY PLANNER

DATE:

MO TU WE
TH FR
SA SU

MOOD:

WEATHER:

APPOINTMENTS

07:00 AM

08:00 AM

09:00 AM

10:00 AM

11:00 AM

12:00 PM

01:00 PM

02:00 PM

03:00 PM

04:00 PM

05:00 PM

06:00 PM

07:00 PM

08:00 PM

09:00 PM

NOTES

WATER INTAKE TOTAL:

DAILY PLANNER

DATE:

MO | TU | WE
TH | FR
SA | SU

MOOD: 😊 🙂 😐 🙁 😢

WEATHER:

APPOINTMENTS

07:00 AM

08:00 AM

09:00 AM

10:00 AM

11:00 AM

12:00 PM

01:00 PM

02:00 PM

03:00 PM

04:00 PM

05:00 PM

06:00 PM

07:00 PM

08:00 PM

09:00 PM

NOTES

WATER INTAKE TOTAL:

DAILY PLANNER

DATE: _____ MO | TU | WE
                        TH | FR
MOOD: 😊 🙂 😐 ☹️ 😢   WEATHER: ☀️ ⛅ ☁️ 🌥️ 🌧️ ❄️   SA | SU

APPOINTMENTS	NOTES
07:00 AM	
08:00 AM	
09:00 AM	
10:00 AM	
11:00 AM	
12:00 PM	
01:00 PM	
02:00 PM	
03:00 PM	
04:00 PM	
05:00 PM	
06:00 PM	
07:00 PM	
08:00 PM	
09:00 PM	

WATER INTAKE TOTAL:
🥛 🥛 🥛 🥛 🥛 🥛 🥛 🥛 🥛 🥛

DAILY PLANNER

DATE:

MO TU WE
TH FR
SA SU

MOOD: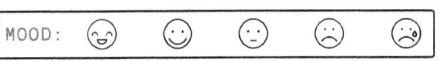

WEATHER:

APPOINTMENTS

07:00 AM

08:00 AM

09:00 AM

10:00 AM

11:00 AM

12:00 PM

01:00 PM

02:00 PM

03:00 PM

04:00 PM

05:00 PM

06:00 PM

07:00 PM

08:00 PM

09:00 PM

NOTES

WATER INTAKE TOTAL:

DAILY PLANNER

DATE:

MO TU WE
TH FR
SA SU

MOOD: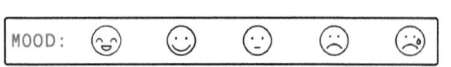

WEATHER:

APPOINTMENTS	NOTES
07:00 AM	
08:00 AM	
09:00 AM	
10:00 AM	
11:00 AM	
12:00 PM	
01:00 PM	
02:00 PM	
03:00 PM	
04:00 PM	
05:00 PM	
06:00 PM	
07:00 PM	
08:00 PM	
09:00 PM	

WATER INTAKE TOTAL:

DAILY PLANNER

DATE: | MO | TU | WE |
| TH | FR |
MOOD: 😊 🙂 😐 🙁 😣 | WEATHER: ☀ ⛅ ☁ 🌦 🌧 ❄ | SA | SU |

APPOINTMENTS

07:00 AM

08:00 AM

09:00 AM

10:00 AM

11:00 AM

12:00 PM

01:00 PM

02:00 PM

03:00 PM

04:00 PM

05:00 PM

06:00 PM

07:00 PM

08:00 PM

09:00 PM

NOTES

WATER INTAKE TOTAL:

DAILY PLANNER

DATE: [ ] MO TU WE
TH FR
MOOD: 🙂 😊 😐 🙁 😞   WEATHER: ☀ ⛅ ☁ 🌦 🌧 ❄   SA SU

APPOINTMENTS	NOTES
07:00 AM	
08:00 AM	
09:00 AM	
10:00 AM	
11:00 AM	
12:00 PM	
01:00 PM	
02:00 PM	
03:00 PM	
04:00 PM	
05:00 PM	
06:00 PM	
07:00 PM	
08:00 PM	
09:00 PM	

WATER INTAKE TOTAL:

DAILY PLANNER

MO TU WE
TH FR
SA SU

MOOD: 😊 🙂 😐 🙁 😞

WEATHER: ☀ ⛅ ☁ 🌬 🌧 ❄

APPOINTMENTS	NOTES
07:00 AM	
08:00 AM	
09:00 AM	
10:00 AM	
11:00 AM	
12:00 PM	
01:00 PM	
02:00 PM	
03:00 PM	
04:00 PM	
05:00 PM	
06:00 PM	
07:00 PM	
08:00 PM	
09:00 PM	

WATER INTAKE TOTAL:

🥛 🥛 🥛 🥛 🥛 🥛 🥛 🥛 🥛 🥛

DAILY PLANNER

DATE: MO | TU | WE
TH | FR
SA | SU

MOOD: 😀   🙂   😐   🙁   😞

WEATHER: ☀ ⛅ ☁ 🌦 🌧 ❄

APPOINTMENTS	NOTES
07:00 AM	
08:00 AM	
09:00 AM	
10:00 AM	
11:00 AM	
12:00 PM	
01:00 PM	
02:00 PM	
03:00 PM	
04:00 PM	
05:00 PM	
06:00 PM	
07:00 PM	
08:00 PM	
09:00 PM	

WATER INTAKE TOTAL:
🥛 🥛 🥛 🥛 🥛 🥛 🥛 🥛 🥛 🥛

DAILY PLANNER

DATE :

MO	TU	WE
TH	FR	
SA	SU	

MOOD : 😊 🙂 😐 🙁 ☹️

WEATHER :

APPOINTMENTS	NOTES
07:00 AM	
08:00 AM	
09:00 AM	
10:00 AM	
11:00 AM	
12:00 PM	
01:00 PM	
02:00 PM	
03:00 PM	
04:00 PM	
05:00 PM	
06:00 PM	
07:00 PM	
08:00 PM	
09:00 PM	

WATER INTAKE TOTAL :

18

DAILY PLANNER

DATE: | MO | TU | WE |
| TH | FR |
| SA | SU |

MOOD: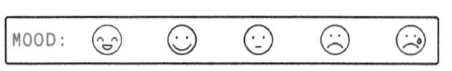

WEATHER:

APPOINTMENTS	NOTES
07:00 AM	
08:00 AM	
09:00 AM	
10:00 AM	
11:00 AM	
12:00 PM	
01:00 PM	
02:00 PM	
03:00 PM	
04:00 PM	
05:00 PM	
06:00 PM	
07:00 PM	
08:00 PM	
09:00 PM	

WATER INTAKE TOTAL:

DAILY PLANNER

DATE:

MO | TU | WE
TH | FR
SA | SU

MOOD: 😊 🙂 😐 🙁 😟

WEATHER:

APPOINTMENTS

07:00 AM

08:00 AM

09:00 AM

10:00 AM

11:00 AM

12:00 PM

01:00 PM

02:00 PM

03:00 PM

04:00 PM

05:00 PM

06:00 PM

07:00 PM

08:00 PM

09:00 PM

NOTES

WATER INTAKE TOTAL:

DAILY PLANNER

DATE: | MO | TU | WE
TH | FR
MOOD: 😊 🙂 😐 🙁 😞   WEATHER: ☀ ⛅ ☁ 🌦 🌧 ❄   SA | SU

APPOINTMENTS

07:00 AM

08:00 AM

09:00 AM

10:00 AM

11:00 AM

12:00 PM

01:00 PM

02:00 PM

03:00 PM

04:00 PM

05:00 PM

06:00 PM

07:00 PM

08:00 PM

09:00 PM

NOTES

WATER INTAKE TOTAL:
🥛 🥛 🥛 🥛 🥛 🥛 🥛 🥛 🥛 🥛

DAILY PLANNER

DATE: | MO | TU | WE
TH | FR
MOOD: 😊 🙂 😐 🙁 😞   WEATHER: ☀ 🌤 ☁ 🌥 🌧 ❄ | SA | SU

APPOINTMENTS	NOTES
07:00 AM	
08:00 AM	
09:00 AM	
10:00 AM	
11:00 AM	
12:00 PM	
01:00 PM	
02:00 PM	
03:00 PM	
04:00 PM	
05:00 PM	
06:00 PM	
07:00 PM	
08:00 PM	
09:00 PM	

WATER INTAKE TOTAL:

🥛 🥛 🥛 🥛 🥛 🥛 🥛 🥛 🥛 🥛

DAILY PLANNER

DATE: | MO | TU | WE
TH | FR
SA | SU

MOOD: 🙂 🙂 😐 🙁 ☹️

WEATHER:

APPOINTMENTS	NOTES
07:00 AM	
08:00 AM	
09:00 AM	
10:00 AM	
11:00 AM	
12:00 PM	
01:00 PM	
02:00 PM	
03:00 PM	
04:00 PM	
05:00 PM	
06:00 PM	
07:00 PM	
08:00 PM	
09:00 PM	

WATER INTAKE TOTAL:

DAILY PLANNER

DATE: _____ | MO | TU | WE |
| TH | FR |

MOOD: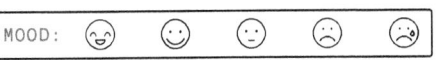

WEATHER: ☀ ⛅ ☁ 🌦 🌧 ❄ | SA | SU |

APPOINTMENTS	NOTES
07:00 AM	
08:00 AM	
09:00 AM	
10:00 AM	
11:00 AM	
12:00 PM	
01:00 PM	
02:00 PM	
03:00 PM	
04:00 PM	
05:00 PM	
06:00 PM	
07:00 PM	
08:00 PM	
09:00 PM	

WATER INTAKE TOTAL:
🥛 🥛 🥛 🥛 🥛 🥛 🥛 🥛 🥛 🥛

DAILY PLANNER

MOOD: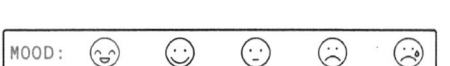

WEATHER:

APPOINTMENTS

07:00 AM
08:00 AM
09:00 AM
10:00 AM
11:00 AM
12:00 PM
01:00 PM
02:00 PM
03:00 PM
04:00 PM
05:00 PM
06:00 PM
07:00 PM
08:00 PM
09:00 PM

NOTES

WATER INTAKE TOTAL:

DAILY PLANNER

MO | TU | WE
TH | FR
SA | SU

MOOD: 😊 🙂 😐 🙁 ☹️

WEATHER: ☀️ 🌤️ ☁️ 🌥️ 🌧️ ❄️

APPOINTMENTS

07:00 AM

08:00 AM

09:00 AM

10:00 AM

11:00 AM

12:00 PM

01:00 PM

02:00 PM

03:00 PM

04:00 PM

05:00 PM

06:00 PM

07:00 PM

08:00 PM

09:00 PM

NOTES

WATER INTAKE TOTAL:

DAILY PLANNER

DATE: [ ] MO TU WE
TH FR
SA SU

MOOD: 😊 🙂 😐 🙁 😞

WEATHER:

APPOINTMENTS

07:00 AM

08:00 AM

09:00 AM

10:00 AM

11:00 AM

12:00 PM

01:00 PM

02:00 PM

03:00 PM

04:00 PM

05:00 PM

06:00 PM

07:00 PM

08:00 PM

09:00 PM

NOTES

WATER INTAKE TOTAL:

27

DAILY PLANNER

DATE: MO   TU   WE   TH   FR   SA   SU

MOOD: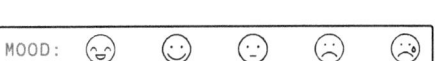

WEATHER:

APPOINTMENTS

07:00 AM

08:00 AM

09:00 AM

10:00 AM

11:00 AM

12:00 PM

01:00 PM

02:00 PM

03:00 PM

04:00 PM

05:00 PM

06:00 PM

07:00 PM

08:00 PM

09:00 PM

NOTES

WATER INTAKE TOTAL:

28

DAILY PLANNER

DATE:

MO | TU | WE
TH | FR
SA | SU

MOOD: 😊 🙂 😐 🙁 ☹️

WEATHER: ☀️ ⛅ ☁️ 🌧️ 🌦️ ❄️

APPOINTMENTS

07:00 AM	
08:00 AM	
09:00 AM	
10:00 AM	
11:00 AM	
12:00 PM	
01:00 PM	
02:00 PM	
03:00 PM	
04:00 PM	
05:00 PM	
06:00 PM	
07:00 PM	
08:00 PM	
09:00 PM	

NOTES

WATER INTAKE TOTAL:

🥤 🥤 🥤 🥤 🥤 🥤 🥤 🥤 🥤 🥤

DAILY PLANNER

DATE: | MO | TU | WE |
| TH | FR |

MOOD: 😊 🙂 😐 🙁 ☹️

WEATHER:  | SA | SU |

APPOINTMENTS	NOTES
07:00 AM	
08:00 AM	
09:00 AM	
10:00 AM	
11:00 AM	
12:00 PM	
01:00 PM	
02:00 PM	
03:00 PM	
04:00 PM	
05:00 PM	
06:00 PM	
07:00 PM	
08:00 PM	
09:00 PM	

WATER INTAKE TOTAL:

🥛 🥛 🥛 🥛 🥛 🥛 🥛 🥛 🥛 🥛

30

DAILY PLANNER

MOOD: 😊 🙂 😐 🙁 ☹️

WEATHER: ☀️ ⛅ ☁️ 🌦️ 🌧️ ❄️

APPOINTMENTS

07:00 AM

08:00 AM

09:00 AM

10:00 AM

11:00 AM

12:00 PM

01:00 PM

02:00 PM

03:00 PM

04:00 PM

05:00 PM

06:00 PM

07:00 PM

08:00 PM

09:00 PM

NOTES

WATER INTAKE TOTAL:

DAILY PLANNER

MOOD: 😄 🙂 😐 🙁 ☹️

WEATHER: ☀️ 🌤️ ☁️ 🌥️ 🌧️ ❄️

APPOINTMENTS

07:00 AM

08:00 AM

09:00 AM

10:00 AM

11:00 AM

12:00 PM

01:00 PM

02:00 PM

03:00 PM

04:00 PM

05:00 PM

06:00 PM

07:00 PM

08:00 PM

09:00 PM

NOTES

WATER INTAKE TOTAL:

DAILY PLANNER

DATE:

MO | TU | WE
TH | FR
SA | SU

MOOD: 😄 🙂 😐 🙁 😣

WEATHER: ☀ ⛅ ☁ 🌤 🌧 ❄

APPOINTMENTS

| 07:00 AM |
| 08:00 AM |
| 09:00 AM |
| 10:00 AM |
| 11:00 AM |
| 12:00 PM |
| 01:00 PM |
| 02:00 PM |
| 03:00 PM |
| 04:00 PM |
| 05:00 PM |
| 06:00 PM |
| 07:00 PM |
| 08:00 PM |
| 09:00 PM |

NOTES

WATER INTAKE TOTAL:

DAILY PLANNER

DATE:

MO | TU | WE
TH | FR
SA | SU

MOOD: 😀 😊 😐 😟 😞

WEATHER:

APPOINTMENTS	NOTES
07:00 AM	
08:00 AM	
09:00 AM	
10:00 AM	
11:00 AM	
12:00 PM	
01:00 PM	
02:00 PM	
03:00 PM	
04:00 PM	
05:00 PM	
06:00 PM	
07:00 PM	
08:00 PM	
09:00 PM	

WATER INTAKE TOTAL:

34

DAILY PLANNER

MOOD: 😉 🙂 😐 🙁 ☹️

WEATHER: ☀️ ⛅ ☁️ 🌦️ 🌧️ ❄️

APPOINTMENTS	NOTES
07:00 AM	
08:00 AM	
09:00 AM	
10:00 AM	
11:00 AM	
12:00 PM	
01:00 PM	
02:00 PM	
03:00 PM	
04:00 PM	
05:00 PM	
06:00 PM	
07:00 PM	
08:00 PM	
09:00 PM	

WATER INTAKE TOTAL:

🥛 🥛 🥛 🥛 🥛 🥛 🥛 🥛 🥛 🥛

DAILY PLANNER

MO TU WE
TH FR
SA SU

MOOD: 😄 ☺ 😐 🙁 😢

WEATHER: ☀ 🌤 ☁ 🌦 🌧 ❄

APPOINTMENTS

07:00 AM

08:00 AM

09:00 AM

10:00 AM

11:00 AM

12:00 PM

01:00 PM

02:00 PM

03:00 PM

04:00 PM

05:00 PM

06:00 PM

07:00 PM

08:00 PM

09:00 PM

NOTES

WATER INTAKE TOTAL:

DAILY PLANNER

MOOD: 😊 🙂 😐 ☹️ 😣

WEATHER: ☀️ ⛅ ☁️ 🌥️ 🌧️ ❄️

APPOINTMENTS

07:00 AM	
08:00 AM	
09:00 AM	
10:00 AM	
11:00 AM	
12:00 PM	
01:00 PM	
02:00 PM	
03:00 PM	
04:00 PM	
05:00 PM	
06:00 PM	
07:00 PM	
08:00 PM	
09:00 PM	

NOTES

WATER INTAKE TOTAL:

🥛 🥛 🥛 🥛 🥛 🥛 🥛 🥛 🥛 🥛

DAILY PLANNER

DATE:

MO	TU	WE
TH	FR
SA	SU

MOOD: 😊 🙂 😐 🙁 ☹️

WEATHER:

APPOINTMENTS

07:00 AM

08:00 AM

09:00 AM

10:00 AM

11:00 AM

12:00 PM

01:00 PM

02:00 PM

03:00 PM

04:00 PM

05:00 PM

06:00 PM

07:00 PM

08:00 PM

09:00 PM

NOTES

WATER INTAKE TOTAL:

DAILY PLANNER

DATE: MO TU WE TH FR SA SU

MOOD: 😄 🙂 😐 🙁 😟

WEATHER: ☀ 🌤 ☁ 🌥 🌧 ❄

APPOINTMENTS	NOTES
07:00 AM	
08:00 AM	
09:00 AM	
10:00 AM	
11:00 AM	
12:00 PM	
01:00 PM	
02:00 PM	
03:00 PM	
04:00 PM	
05:00 PM	
06:00 PM	
07:00 PM	
08:00 PM	
09:00 PM	

WATER INTAKE TOTAL:

DAILY PLANNER

DATE: _____

MO TU WE
TH FR
SA SU

MOOD: ☺ ☺ ☺ ☹ ☹

WEATHER: ☼ ⛅ ☁ 🌦 🌧 ❄

APPOINTMENTS
07:00 AM
08:00 AM
09:00 AM
10:00 AM
11:00 AM
12:00 PM
01:00 PM
02:00 PM
03:00 PM
04:00 PM
05:00 PM
06:00 PM
07:00 PM
08:00 PM
09:00 PM

NOTES

WATER INTAKE TOTAL:

🥛 🥛 🥛 🥛 🥛 🥛 🥛 🥛 🥛 🥛

DAILY PLANNER

DATE: | MO | TU | WE |
| TH | FR |
| SA | SU |

MOOD: 😃 🙂 😐 😟 😢

WEATHER:

APPOINTMENTS	NOTES
07:00 AM	
08:00 AM	
09:00 AM	
10:00 AM	
11:00 AM	
12:00 PM	
01:00 PM	
02:00 PM	
03:00 PM	
04:00 PM	
05:00 PM	
06:00 PM	
07:00 PM	
08:00 PM	
09:00 PM	

WATER INTAKE TOTAL:

DAILY PLANNER

DATE :

MO	TU	WE
TH	FR
SA	SU

MOOD : 😀 🙂 😐 🙁 😞

WEATHER :

APPOINTMENTS	NOTES
07:00 AM	
08:00 AM	
09:00 AM	
10:00 AM	
11:00 AM	
12:00 PM	
01:00 PM	
02:00 PM	
03:00 PM	
04:00 PM	
05:00 PM	
06:00 PM	
07:00 PM	
08:00 PM	
09:00 PM	

WATER INTAKE TOTAL :

DAILY PLANNER

MOOD: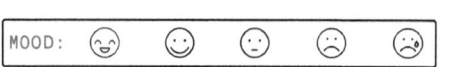

WEATHER:

APPOINTMENTS	NOTES
07:00 AM	
08:00 AM	
09:00 AM	
10:00 AM	
11:00 AM	
12:00 PM	
01:00 PM	
02:00 PM	
03:00 PM	
04:00 PM	
05:00 PM	
06:00 PM	
07:00 PM	
08:00 PM	
09:00 PM	

WATER INTAKE TOTAL:

DAILY PLANNER

DATE:

MO | TU | WE
TH | FR
SA | SU

MOOD: 😊 🙂 😐 🙁 ☹️

WEATHER:

APPOINTMENTS	NOTES
07:00 AM	
08:00 AM	
09:00 AM	
10:00 AM	
11:00 AM	
12:00 PM	
01:00 PM	
02:00 PM	
03:00 PM	
04:00 PM	
05:00 PM	
06:00 PM	
07:00 PM	
08:00 PM	
09:00 PM	

WATER INTAKE TOTAL:

DAILY PLANNER

MOOD: 😊 🙂 😐 🙁 ☹️

WEATHER: ☀️ ⛅ ☁️ 🌧️ ❄️

APPOINTMENTS	NOTES
07:00 AM	
08:00 AM	
09:00 AM	
10:00 AM	
11:00 AM	
12:00 PM	
01:00 PM	
02:00 PM	
03:00 PM	
04:00 PM	
05:00 PM	
06:00 PM	
07:00 PM	
08:00 PM	
09:00 PM	

WATER INTAKE TOTAL:

45

DAILY PLANNER

MO TU WE
TH FR
SA SU

MOOD: 😊 🙂 😐 🙁 😞

WEATHER: ☀️ ⛅ ☁️ 🌬️ 🌧️ ❄️

APPOINTMENTS	NOTES
07:00 AM	
08:00 AM	
09:00 AM	
10:00 AM	
11:00 AM	
12:00 PM	
01:00 PM	
02:00 PM	
03:00 PM	
04:00 PM	
05:00 PM	
06:00 PM	
07:00 PM	
08:00 PM	
09:00 PM	

WATER INTAKE TOTAL:

DAILY PLANNER

DATE: | MO | TU | WE |
| TH | FR |

MOOD: 😄 🙂 😐 🙁 😞

WEATHER: | SA | SU |

APPOINTMENTS	NOTES
07:00 AM	
08:00 AM	
09:00 AM	
10:00 AM	
11:00 AM	
12:00 PM	
01:00 PM	
02:00 PM	
03:00 PM	
04:00 PM	
05:00 PM	
06:00 PM	
07:00 PM	
08:00 PM	
09:00 PM	

WATER INTAKE TOTAL:

DAILY PLANNER

DATE: | MO | TU | WE |
| TH | FR |
| SA | SU |

MOOD: 😊 🙂 😐 🙁 😞

WEATHER: ☀ ⛅ ☁ 🌬 🌧 ❄

APPOINTMENTS	NOTES
07:00 AM	
08:00 AM	
09:00 AM	
10:00 AM	
11:00 AM	
12:00 PM	
01:00 PM	
02:00 PM	
03:00 PM	
04:00 PM	
05:00 PM	
06:00 PM	
07:00 PM	
08:00 PM	
09:00 PM	

WATER INTAKE TOTAL:

DAILY PLANNER

MOOD: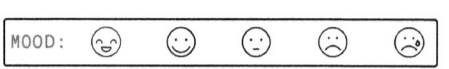

WEATHER:

APPOINTMENTS

07:00 AM	
08:00 AM	
09:00 AM	
10:00 AM	
11:00 AM	
12:00 PM	
01:00 PM	
02:00 PM	
03:00 PM	
04:00 PM	
05:00 PM	
06:00 PM	
07:00 PM	
08:00 PM	
09:00 PM	

NOTES

WATER INTAKE TOTAL:

DAILY PLANNER

MO TU WE
TH FR
MOOD: 😊 🙂 😐 🙁 😞   WEATHER: ☀ ⛅ ☁ 🌬 🌧 ❄   SA SU

APPOINTMENTS

07:00 AM

08:00 AM

09:00 AM

10:00 AM

11:00 AM

12:00 PM

01:00 PM

02:00 PM

03:00 PM

04:00 PM

05:00 PM

06:00 PM

07:00 PM

08:00 PM

09:00 PM

NOTES

WATER INTAKE TOTAL:
🥛 🥛 🥛 🥛 🥛 🥛 🥛 🥛 🥛 🥛

50

DAILY PLANNER

DATE: MO TU WE TH FR SA SU

MOOD: 😊 🙂 😐 🙁 😞

WEATHER:

APPOINTMENTS

07:00 AM

08:00 AM

09:00 AM

10:00 AM

11:00 AM

12:00 PM

01:00 PM

02:00 PM

03:00 PM

04:00 PM

05:00 PM

06:00 PM

07:00 PM

08:00 PM

09:00 PM

NOTES

WATER INTAKE TOTAL:

DAILY PLANNER

DATE:

MO | TU | WE
TH | FR
SA | SU

MOOD: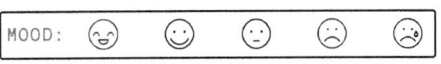

WEATHER:

APPOINTMENTS	NOTES
07:00 AM	
08:00 AM	
09:00 AM	
10:00 AM	
11:00 AM	
12:00 PM	
01:00 PM	
02:00 PM	
03:00 PM	
04:00 PM	
05:00 PM	
06:00 PM	
07:00 PM	
08:00 PM	
09:00 PM	

WATER INTAKE TOTAL:

DAILY PLANNER

MOOD: 😊 🙂 😐 🙁 😢

WEATHER: ☀️ ⛅ ☁️ 🌦️ 🌧️ ❄️

APPOINTMENTS	NOTES
07:00 AM	
08:00 AM	
09:00 AM	
10:00 AM	
11:00 AM	
12:00 PM	
01:00 PM	
02:00 PM	
03:00 PM	
04:00 PM	
05:00 PM	
06:00 PM	
07:00 PM	
08:00 PM	
09:00 PM	

WATER INTAKE TOTAL:

DAILY PLANNER

DATE:

MO TU WE
TH FR
SA SU

MOOD: 😊 🙂 😐 🙁 😞

WEATHER:

APPOINTMENTS

07:00 AM

08:00 AM

09:00 AM

10:00 AM

11:00 AM

12:00 PM

01:00 PM

02:00 PM

03:00 PM

04:00 PM

05:00 PM

06:00 PM

07:00 PM

08:00 PM

09:00 PM

NOTES

WATER INTAKE TOTAL:

DAILY PLANNER

DATE: | MO | TU | WE
TH | FR
MOOD: 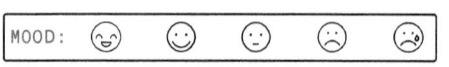 **WEATHER:** | SA | SU

APPOINTMENTS	NOTES
07:00 AM	
08:00 AM	
09:00 AM	
10:00 AM	
11:00 AM	
12:00 PM	
01:00 PM	
02:00 PM	
03:00 PM	
04:00 PM	
05:00 PM	
06:00 PM	
07:00 PM	
08:00 PM	
09:00 PM	

WATER INTAKE TOTAL:

DAILY PLANNER

DATE:

MO | TU | WE
TH | FR
SA | SU

MOOD:

WEATHER:

APPOINTMENTS

07:00 AM

08:00 AM

09:00 AM

10:00 AM

11:00 AM

12:00 PM

01:00 PM

02:00 PM

03:00 PM

04:00 PM

05:00 PM

06:00 PM

07:00 PM

08:00 PM

09:00 PM

NOTES

WATER INTAKE TOTAL:

DAILY PLANNER

MOOD: 😊   🙂   😐   🙁   😢

WEATHER:

APPOINTMENTS

07:00 AM	
08:00 AM	
09:00 AM	
10:00 AM	
11:00 AM	
12:00 PM	
01:00 PM	
02:00 PM	
03:00 PM	
04:00 PM	
05:00 PM	
06:00 PM	
07:00 PM	
08:00 PM	
09:00 PM	

NOTES

WATER INTAKE TOTAL:

DAILY PLANNER

DATE:

MO TU WE
TH FR
SA SU

MOOD: 😊 🙂 😐 🙁 😞

WEATHER:

APPOINTMENTS

07:00 AM

08:00 AM

09:00 AM

10:00 AM

11:00 AM

12:00 PM

01:00 PM

02:00 PM

03:00 PM

04:00 PM

05:00 PM

06:00 PM

07:00 PM

08:00 PM

09:00 PM

NOTES

WATER INTAKE TOTAL:

DAILY PLANNER

DATE: _____ MO | TU | WE

TH | FR

MOOD: 😄 🙂 😐 🙁 😢   WEATHER: ☀️ ⛅ ☁️ 🌦️ 🌧️ ❄️   SA | SU

APPOINTMENTS

07:00 AM
08:00 AM
09:00 AM
10:00 AM
11:00 AM
12:00 PM
01:00 PM
02:00 PM
03:00 PM
04:00 PM
05:00 PM
06:00 PM
07:00 PM
08:00 PM
09:00 PM

NOTES

WATER INTAKE TOTAL:

DAILY PLANNER

MOOD :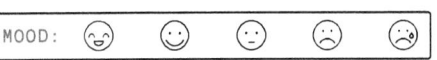

WEATHER :

APPOINTMENTS	NOTES
07:00 AM	
08:00 AM	
09:00 AM	
10:00 AM	
11:00 AM	
12:00 PM	
01:00 PM	
02:00 PM	
03:00 PM	
04:00 PM	
05:00 PM	
06:00 PM	
07:00 PM	
08:00 PM	
09:00 PM	

WATER INTAKE TOTAL :

DAILY PLANNER

DATE: | MO | TU | WE
TH | FR
SA | SU

MOOD: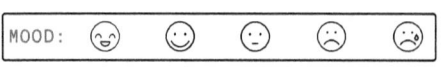

WEATHER:

APPOINTMENTS	NOTES
07:00 AM	
08:00 AM	
09:00 AM	
10:00 AM	
11:00 AM	
12:00 PM	
01:00 PM	
02:00 PM	
03:00 PM	
04:00 PM	
05:00 PM	
06:00 PM	
07:00 PM	
08:00 PM	
09:00 PM	

WATER INTAKE TOTAL:

DAILY PLANNER

DATE:

MOOD:

WEATHER:

APPOINTMENTS

07:00 AM

08:00 AM

09:00 AM

10:00 AM

11:00 AM

12:00 PM

01:00 PM

02:00 PM

03:00 PM

04:00 PM

05:00 PM

06:00 PM

07:00 PM

08:00 PM

09:00 PM

NOTES

WATER INTAKE TOTAL:

62

DAILY PLANNER

DATE: | MO | TU | WE
TH | FR
MOOD: 😊 🙂 😐 🙁 😞   WEATHER: ☀ ⛅ ☁ 🌦 🌧 ❄   SA | SU

APPOINTMENTS	NOTES
07:00 AM	
08:00 AM	
09:00 AM	
10:00 AM	
11:00 AM	
12:00 PM	
01:00 PM	
02:00 PM	
03:00 PM	
04:00 PM	
05:00 PM	
06:00 PM	
07:00 PM	
08:00 PM	
09:00 PM	

WATER INTAKE TOTAL:
🥛 🥛 🥛 🥛 🥛 🥛 🥛 🥛 🥛 🥛

DAILY PLANNER

DATE:

MO | TU | WE
TH | FR
SA | SU

MOOD:

WEATHER:

APPOINTMENTS	NOTES
07:00 AM	
08:00 AM	
09:00 AM	
10:00 AM	
11:00 AM	
12:00 PM	
01:00 PM	
02:00 PM	
03:00 PM	
04:00 PM	
05:00 PM	
06:00 PM	
07:00 PM	
08:00 PM	
09:00 PM	

WATER INTAKE TOTAL:

DAILY PLANNER

DATE:

MO | TU | WE
TH | FR
SA | SU

MOOD: 😊 😊 😐 🙁 😞

WEATHER: ☀️ 🌤️ ☁️ 🌥️ 🌧️ ❄️

APPOINTMENTS

07:00 AM

08:00 AM

09:00 AM

10:00 AM

11:00 AM

12:00 PM

01:00 PM

02:00 PM

03:00 PM

04:00 PM

05:00 PM

06:00 PM

07:00 PM

08:00 PM

09:00 PM

NOTES

WATER INTAKE TOTAL:

DAILY PLANNER

DATE: | MO | TU | WE
TH | FR

MOOD: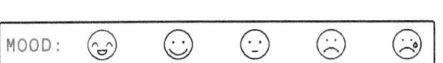

WEATHER: ☀ ⛅ ☁ 🌬 🌧 ❄ | SA | SU

APPOINTMENTS	NOTES
07:00 AM	
08:00 AM	
09:00 AM	
10:00 AM	
11:00 AM	
12:00 PM	
01:00 PM	
02:00 PM	
03:00 PM	
04:00 PM	
05:00 PM	
06:00 PM	
07:00 PM	
08:00 PM	
09:00 PM	

WATER INTAKE TOTAL:
🥛 🥛 🥛 🥛 🥛 🥛 🥛 🥛 🥛 🥛

DAILY PLANNER

DATE: | MO | TU | WE
TH | FR
WEATHER: 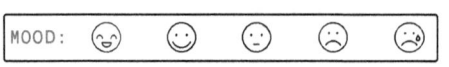 | SA | SU

MOOD:

APPOINTMENTS	NOTES
07:00 AM	
08:00 AM	
09:00 AM	
10:00 AM	
11:00 AM	
12:00 PM	
01:00 PM	
02:00 PM	
03:00 PM	
04:00 PM	
05:00 PM	
06:00 PM	
07:00 PM	
08:00 PM	
09:00 PM	

WATER INTAKE TOTAL:

DAILY PLANNER

DATE: _____

MO	TU	WE
TH	FR	
SA	SU	

MOOD: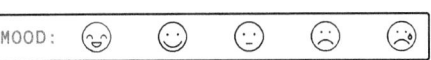

WEATHER: ☀ ⛅ ☁ 🌦 🌧 ❄

APPOINTMENTS	NOTES
07:00 AM	
08:00 AM	
09:00 AM	
10:00 AM	
11:00 AM	
12:00 PM	
01:00 PM	
02:00 PM	
03:00 PM	
04:00 PM	
05:00 PM	
06:00 PM	
07:00 PM	
08:00 PM	
09:00 PM	

WATER INTAKE TOTAL:

⊔ ⊔ ⊔ ⊔ ⊔ ⊔ ⊔ ⊔ ⊔ ⊔

DAILY PLANNER

DATE:

MO | TU | WE
TH | FR
SA | SU

MOOD: 😄 🙂 😐 🙁 😞

WEATHER:

APPOINTMENTS	NOTES
07:00 AM	
08:00 AM	
09:00 AM	
10:00 AM	
11:00 AM	
12:00 PM	
01:00 PM	
02:00 PM	
03:00 PM	
04:00 PM	
05:00 PM	
06:00 PM	
07:00 PM	
08:00 PM	
09:00 PM	

WATER INTAKE TOTAL:

DAILY PLANNER

DATE: _____ | MO | TU | WE |
                     | TH | FR |
MOOD: 😄 🙂 😐 🙁 😞   WEATHER: ☀ ⛅ ☁ 🌬 🌧 ❄ | SA | SU |

APPOINTMENTS

07:00 AM

08:00 AM

09:00 AM

10:00 AM

11:00 AM

12:00 PM

01:00 PM

02:00 PM

03:00 PM

04:00 PM

05:00 PM

06:00 PM

07:00 PM

08:00 PM

09:00 PM

NOTES

WATER INTAKE TOTAL:
🥛 🥛 🥛 🥛 🥛 🥛 🥛 🥛 🥛 🥛

70

DAILY PLANNER

DATE: | MO | TU | WE
TH | FR
SA | SU

MOOD: 😃 ☺ 😐 ☹ 😫

WEATHER:

APPOINTMENTS

07:00 AM

08:00 AM

09:00 AM

10:00 AM

11:00 AM

12:00 PM

01:00 PM

02:00 PM

03:00 PM

04:00 PM

05:00 PM

06:00 PM

07:00 PM

08:00 PM

09:00 PM

NOTES

WATER INTAKE TOTAL:

71

DAILY PLANNER

DATE: | MO | TU | WE |
| TH | FR |

MOOD: 😊 😊 😐 🙁 😞   WEATHER: ☀ ⛅ ☁ 🌬 🌧 ❄ | SA | SU |

APPOINTMENTS

07:00 AM

08:00 AM

09:00 AM

10:00 AM

11:00 AM

12:00 PM

01:00 PM

02:00 PM

03:00 PM

04:00 PM

05:00 PM

06:00 PM

07:00 PM

08:00 PM

09:00 PM

NOTES

WATER INTAKE TOTAL:

DAILY PLANNER

DATE: | MO | TU | WE
| TH | FR
MOOD: 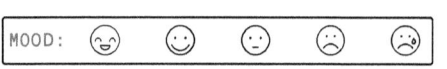 WEATHER: ☀ ⛅ ☁ 🌬 🌧 ❄ | SA | SU

APPOINTMENTS	NOTES
07:00 AM	
08:00 AM	
09:00 AM	
10:00 AM	
11:00 AM	
12:00 PM	
01:00 PM	
02:00 PM	
03:00 PM	
04:00 PM	
05:00 PM	
06:00 PM	
07:00 PM	
08:00 PM	
09:00 PM	

WATER INTAKE TOTAL:
⊔ ⊔ ⊔ ⊔ ⊔ ⊔ ⊔ ⊔ ⊔ ⊔

DAILY PLANNER

DATE:

MO TU WE
TH FR
SA SU

MOOD: 😊 🙂 😐 🙁 😟

WEATHER: ☀ 🌤 ☁ 🌬 🌧 ❄

APPOINTMENTS

07:00 AM

08:00 AM

09:00 AM

10:00 AM

11:00 AM

12:00 PM

01:00 PM

02:00 PM

03:00 PM

04:00 PM

05:00 PM

06:00 PM

07:00 PM

08:00 PM

09:00 PM

NOTES

WATER INTAKE TOTAL:

DAILY PLANNER

MOOD: 😊 🙂 😐 🙁 😢

WEATHER: ☀ 🌤 ☁ 🌥 🌧 ❄

APPOINTMENTS	NOTES
07:00 AM	
08:00 AM	
09:00 AM	
10:00 AM	
11:00 AM	
12:00 PM	
01:00 PM	
02:00 PM	
03:00 PM	
04:00 PM	
05:00 PM	
06:00 PM	
07:00 PM	
08:00 PM	
09:00 PM	

WATER INTAKE TOTAL:

DAILY PLANNER

DATE:

MO | TU | WE
TH | FR
SA | SU

MOOD: 😊 🙂 😐 🙁 ☹️

WEATHER: ☀️ ⛅ ☁️ 🌦️ 🌧️ ❄️

APPOINTMENTS

07:00 AM

08:00 AM

09:00 AM

10:00 AM

11:00 AM

12:00 PM

01:00 PM

02:00 PM

03:00 PM

04:00 PM

05:00 PM

06:00 PM

07:00 PM

08:00 PM

09:00 PM

NOTES

WATER INTAKE TOTAL:

DAILY PLANNER

MO TU WE
TH FR
SA SU

MOOD: 😊 😊 😐 😞 😢

WEATHER: ☀ ⛅ ☁ 🌧 🌦 ❄

APPOINTMENTS	NOTES
07:00 AM	
08:00 AM	
09:00 AM	
10:00 AM	
11:00 AM	
12:00 PM	
01:00 PM	
02:00 PM	
03:00 PM	
04:00 PM	
05:00 PM	
06:00 PM	
07:00 PM	
08:00 PM	
09:00 PM	

WATER INTAKE TOTAL:

DAILY PLANNER

DATE : [   ]

MO TU WE
TH FR
SA SU

MOOD :

WEATHER :

APPOINTMENTS	NOTES
07:00 AM	
08:00 AM	
09:00 AM	
10:00 AM	
11:00 AM	
12:00 PM	
01:00 PM	
02:00 PM	
03:00 PM	
04:00 PM	
05:00 PM	
06:00 PM	
07:00 PM	
08:00 PM	
09:00 PM	

WATER INTAKE TOTAL :

78

DAILY PLANNER

DATE: MO TU WE
TH FR
SA SU

MOOD: 😄 🙂 😐 🙁 ☹️

WEATHER: ☀️ ⛅ ☁️ 🌦️ 🌧️ ❄️

APPOINTMENTS

07:00 AM	
08:00 AM	
09:00 AM	
10:00 AM	
11:00 AM	
12:00 PM	
01:00 PM	
02:00 PM	
03:00 PM	
04:00 PM	
05:00 PM	
06:00 PM	
07:00 PM	
08:00 PM	
09:00 PM	

NOTES

WATER INTAKE TOTAL:
🥛 🥛 🥛 🥛 🥛 🥛 🥛 🥛 🥛 🥛

DAILY PLANNER

MOOD: 😊 🙂 😐 🙁 ☹️

WEATHER: ☀️ ⛅ ☁️ 🌧️ 🌦️ ❄️

APPOINTMENTS

07:00 AM

08:00 AM

09:00 AM

10:00 AM

11:00 AM

12:00 PM

01:00 PM

02:00 PM

03:00 PM

04:00 PM

05:00 PM

06:00 PM

07:00 PM

08:00 PM

09:00 PM

NOTES

WATER INTAKE TOTAL:

80

DAILY PLANNER

MO | TU | WE
TH | FR
SA | SU

MOOD: 😄 🙂 😐 🙁 😣

WEATHER: ☀️ ⛅ ☁️ 🌥️ 🌧️ ❄️

APPOINTMENTS

07:00 AM

08:00 AM

09:00 AM

10:00 AM

11:00 AM

12:00 PM

01:00 PM

02:00 PM

03:00 PM

04:00 PM

05:00 PM

06:00 PM

07:00 PM

08:00 PM

09:00 PM

NOTES

WATER INTAKE TOTAL:

DAILY PLANNER

DATE: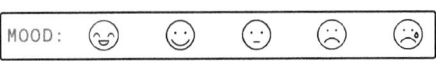

MO TU WE
TH FR
SA SU

MOOD: 😄 🙂 😐 🙁 😞

WEATHER: ☀️ ⛅ ☁️ 🌬️ 🌧️ ❄️

APPOINTMENTS	NOTES
07:00 AM	
08:00 AM	
09:00 AM	
10:00 AM	
11:00 AM	
12:00 PM	
01:00 PM	
02:00 PM	
03:00 PM	
04:00 PM	
05:00 PM	
06:00 PM	
07:00 PM	
08:00 PM	
09:00 PM	

WATER INTAKE TOTAL:

🥛 🥛 🥛 🥛 🥛 🥛 🥛 🥛 🥛 🥛

DAILY PLANNER

MO TU WE
TH FR
SA SU

MOOD: 😊 🙂 😐 🙁 😣

WEATHER: ☀️ ⛅ ☁️ 🌥️ 🌧️ ❄️

APPOINTMENTS	NOTES
07:00 AM	
08:00 AM	
09:00 AM	
10:00 AM	
11:00 AM	
12:00 PM	
01:00 PM	
02:00 PM	
03:00 PM	
04:00 PM	
05:00 PM	
06:00 PM	
07:00 PM	
08:00 PM	
09:00 PM	

WATER INTAKE TOTAL:

DAILY PLANNER

DATE:

MO	TU	WE
TH	FR
SA	SU

MOOD: 😊 🙂 😐 🙁 ☹️

WEATHER:

APPOINTMENTS

07:00 AM

08:00 AM

09:00 AM

10:00 AM

11:00 AM

12:00 PM

01:00 PM

02:00 PM

03:00 PM

04:00 PM

05:00 PM

06:00 PM

07:00 PM

08:00 PM

09:00 PM

NOTES

WATER INTAKE TOTAL:

DAILY PLANNER

DATE:

MO TU WE TH FR SA SU

MOOD: 😊 🙂 😐 🙁 ☹️

WEATHER:

APPOINTMENTS
07:00 AM
08:00 AM
09:00 AM
10:00 AM
11:00 AM
12:00 PM
01:00 PM
02:00 PM
03:00 PM
04:00 PM
05:00 PM
06:00 PM
07:00 PM
08:00 PM
09:00 PM

NOTES

WATER INTAKE TOTAL:

DAILY PLANNER

DATE:

MO	TU	WE
TH	FR
SA	SU

MOOD: 😄 🙂 😐 🙁 😣

WEATHER: ☀️ ⛅ ☁️ 🌦️ 🌧️ ❄️

APPOINTMENTS	NOTES
07:00 AM	
08:00 AM	
09:00 AM	
10:00 AM	
11:00 AM	
12:00 PM	
01:00 PM	
02:00 PM	
03:00 PM	
04:00 PM	
05:00 PM	
06:00 PM	
07:00 PM	
08:00 PM	
09:00 PM	

WATER INTAKE TOTAL:

DAILY PLANNER

DATE:

MO TU WE
TH FR
SA SU

MOOD:

WEATHER:

APPOINTMENTS

07:00 AM

08:00 AM

09:00 AM

10:00 AM

11:00 AM

12:00 PM

01:00 PM

02:00 PM

03:00 PM

04:00 PM

05:00 PM

06:00 PM

07:00 PM

08:00 PM

09:00 PM

NOTES

WATER INTAKE TOTAL:

DAILY PLANNER

DATE:

MO TU WE
TH FR
SA SU

MOOD:

WEATHER:

APPOINTMENTS

07:00 AM

08:00 AM

09:00 AM

10:00 AM

11:00 AM

12:00 PM

01:00 PM

02:00 PM

03:00 PM

04:00 PM

05:00 PM

06:00 PM

07:00 PM

08:00 PM

09:00 PM

NOTES

WATER INTAKE TOTAL:

DAILY PLANNER

DATE: | MO | TU | WE | TH | FR | SA | SU

MOOD: 😊 🙂 😐 🙁 😞

WEATHER: ☀ ⛅ ☁ 🌦 🌧 ❄

APPOINTMENTS

07:00 AM
08:00 AM
09:00 AM
10:00 AM
11:00 AM
12:00 PM
01:00 PM
02:00 PM
03:00 PM
04:00 PM
05:00 PM
06:00 PM
07:00 PM
08:00 PM
09:00 PM

NOTES

WATER INTAKE TOTAL:

DAILY PLANNER

DATE :

MO | TU | WE
TH | FR
SA | SU

MOOD :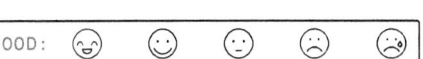

WEATHER :

APPOINTMENTS

07:00 AM

08:00 AM

09:00 AM

10:00 AM

11:00 AM

12:00 PM

01:00 PM

02:00 PM

03:00 PM

04:00 PM

05:00 PM

06:00 PM

07:00 PM

08:00 PM

09:00 PM

NOTES

WATER INTAKE TOTAL :

DAILY PLANNER

DATE: | MO | TU | WE
TH | FR
SA | SU

MOOD: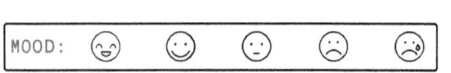

WEATHER:

APPOINTMENTS	NOTES
07:00 AM	
08:00 AM	
09:00 AM	
10:00 AM	
11:00 AM	
12:00 PM	
01:00 PM	
02:00 PM	
03:00 PM	
04:00 PM	
05:00 PM	
06:00 PM	
07:00 PM	
08:00 PM	
09:00 PM	

WATER INTAKE TOTAL:

DAILY PLANNER

DATE: | MO | TU | WE
TH | FR
SA | SU

MOOD: 😊 🙂 😐 ☹️ 😞

WEATHER:

APPOINTMENTS

07:00 AM

08:00 AM

09:00 AM

10:00 AM

11:00 AM

12:00 PM

01:00 PM

02:00 PM

03:00 PM

04:00 PM

05:00 PM

06:00 PM

07:00 PM

08:00 PM

09:00 PM

NOTES

WATER INTAKE TOTAL:

DAILY PLANNER

DATE:

MO | TU | WE
TH | FR
SA | SU

MOOD: 😊 🙂 😐 🙁 ☹️

WEATHER:

APPOINTMENTS	NOTES
07:00 AM	
08:00 AM	
09:00 AM	
10:00 AM	
11:00 AM	
12:00 PM	
01:00 PM	
02:00 PM	
03:00 PM	
04:00 PM	
05:00 PM	
06:00 PM	
07:00 PM	
08:00 PM	
09:00 PM	

WATER INTAKE TOTAL:

DAILY PLANNER

MOOD: 😊 🙂 😐 🙁 😞

WEATHER:

APPOINTMENTS

07:00 AM	
08:00 AM	
09:00 AM	
10:00 AM	
11:00 AM	
12:00 PM	
01:00 PM	
02:00 PM	
03:00 PM	
04:00 PM	
05:00 PM	
06:00 PM	
07:00 PM	
08:00 PM	
09:00 PM	

NOTES

WATER INTAKE TOTAL:
🥛 🥛 🥛 🥛 🥛 🥛 🥛 🥛 🥛 🥛

DAILY PLANNER

MOOD:　😊　🙂　😐　🙁　😞

WEATHER:　☀　⛅　☁　🌦　🌧　❄

APPOINTMENTS	NOTES
07:00 AM	
08:00 AM	
09:00 AM	
10:00 AM	
11:00 AM	
12:00 PM	
01:00 PM	
02:00 PM	
03:00 PM	
04:00 PM	
05:00 PM	
06:00 PM	
07:00 PM	
08:00 PM	
09:00 PM	

WATER INTAKE TOTAL:

DAILY PLANNER

MO TU WE
TH FR
SA SU

MOOD: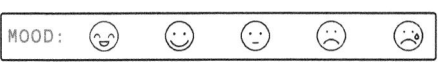

WEATHER:

APPOINTMENTS	NOTES
07:00 AM	
08:00 AM	
09:00 AM	
10:00 AM	
11:00 AM	
12:00 PM	
01:00 PM	
02:00 PM	
03:00 PM	
04:00 PM	
05:00 PM	
06:00 PM	
07:00 PM	
08:00 PM	
09:00 PM	

WATER INTAKE TOTAL:

DAILY PLANNER

DATE: [ ] MO | TU | WE
TH | FR
SA | SU

MOOD: 😊 🙂 😐 🙁 😣

WEATHER:

APPOINTMENTS	NOTES
07:00 AM	
08:00 AM	
09:00 AM	
10:00 AM	
11:00 AM	
12:00 PM	
01:00 PM	
02:00 PM	
03:00 PM	
04:00 PM	
05:00 PM	
06:00 PM	
07:00 PM	
08:00 PM	
09:00 PM	

WATER INTAKE TOTAL:

95

DAILY PLANNER

DATE: | MO | TU | WE
| TH | FR

MOOD: 😊 🙂 😐 🙁 😞

WEATHER: ☀ ⛅ ☁ 🌥 🌧 ❄ | SA | SU

APPOINTMENTS

07:00 AM

08:00 AM

09:00 AM

10:00 AM

11:00 AM

12:00 PM

01:00 PM

02:00 PM

03:00 PM

04:00 PM

05:00 PM

06:00 PM

07:00 PM

08:00 PM

09:00 PM

NOTES

WATER INTAKE TOTAL:

🥛 🥛 🥛 🥛 🥛 🥛 🥛 🥛 🥛 🥛

95

DAILY PLANNER

DATE:

MO | TU | W
TH | F
SA | S

MOOD: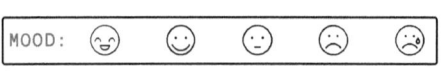

WEATHER:

APPOINTMENTS

07:00 AM
08:00 AM
09:00 AM
10:00 AM
11:00 AM
12:00 PM
01:00 PM
02:00 PM
03:00 PM
04:00 PM
05:00 PM
06:00 PM
07:00 PM
08:00 PM
09:00 PM

NOTES

WATER INTAKE TOTAL:

DAILY PLANNER

DATE: ⬜ MO TU WE
TH FR
MOOD: 😃 🙂 😐 🙁 ☹️　　WEATHER: ☀️ ⛅ ☁️ 🌫️ 🌧️ ❄️ SA SU

APPOINTMENTS

07:00 AM

08:00 AM

09:00 AM

10:00 AM

11:00 AM

12:00 PM

01:00 PM

02:00 PM

03:00 PM

04:00 PM

05:00 PM

06:00 PM

07:00 PM

08:00 PM

09:00 PM

NOTES

WATER INTAKE TOTAL:
🥛 🥛 🥛 🥛 🥛 🥛 🥛 🥛 🥛 🥛

95

DAILY PLANNER

DATE: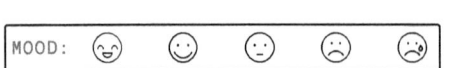

MO	TU	WI
TH	FI
SA	SI

MOOD: 😀 ☺ ☺ ☹ ☹

WEATHER: ☀ ⛅ ☁ 🌬 🌧 ❄

APPOINTMENTS	NOTES
07:00 AM	
08:00 AM	
09:00 AM	
10:00 AM	
11:00 AM	
12:00 PM	
01:00 PM	
02:00 PM	
03:00 PM	
04:00 PM	
05:00 PM	
06:00 PM	
07:00 PM	
08:00 PM	
09:00 PM	

WATER INTAKE TOTAL:

🥛 🥛 🥛 🥛 🥛 🥛 🥛 🥛 🥛 🥛

96

DAILY PLANNER

DATE:

MO TU WE
TH FR
SA SU

MOOD: 🙂 🙂 😐 🙁 ☹️

WEATHER:

APPOINTMENTS

07:00 AM

08:00 AM

09:00 AM

10:00 AM

11:00 AM

12:00 PM

01:00 PM

02:00 PM

03:00 PM

04:00 PM

05:00 PM

06:00 PM

07:00 PM

08:00 PM

09:00 PM

NOTES

WATER INTAKE TOTAL:

95

DAILY PLANNER

DATE: | MO | TU | WE
TH | FR
SA | SU

MOOD: 😄 🙂 😐 🙁 😞

WEATHER: ☀ 🌤 ☁ 🌥 🌧 ❄

APPOINTMENTS	NOTES
07:00 AM	
08:00 AM	
09:00 AM	
10:00 AM	
11:00 AM	
12:00 PM	
01:00 PM	
02:00 PM	
03:00 PM	
04:00 PM	
05:00 PM	
06:00 PM	
07:00 PM	
08:00 PM	
09:00 PM	

WATER INTAKE TOTAL:
🥛 🥛 🥛 🥛 🥛 🥛 🥛 🥛 🥛 🥛

DAILY PLANNER

DATE: _____

MO TU WE
TH FR
SA SU

MOOD: 😆 🙂 😐 🙁 😣

WEATHER: ☀ ⛅ ☁ 🌦 🌧 ❄

APPOINTMENTS	NOTES
07:00 AM	
08:00 AM	
09:00 AM	
10:00 AM	
11:00 AM	
12:00 PM	
01:00 PM	
02:00 PM	
03:00 PM	
04:00 PM	
05:00 PM	
06:00 PM	
07:00 PM	
08:00 PM	
09:00 PM	

WATER INTAKE TOTAL:

95

DAILY PLANNER

DATE: | MO | TU | W

| TH | F
MOOD: 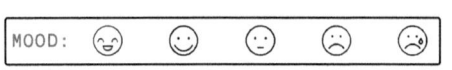 | WEATHER: | SA | S

APPOINTMENTS

07:00 AM

08:00 AM

09:00 AM

10:00 AM

11:00 AM

12:00 PM

01:00 PM

02:00 PM

03:00 PM

04:00 PM

05:00 PM

06:00 PM

07:00 PM

08:00 PM

09:00 PM

NOTES

WATER INTAKE TOTAL:

96

DAILY PLANNER

DATE: | MO | TU | WE |
| TH | FR |

MOOD: 😊 🙂 😐 🙁 😞

WEATHER: ☀️ ⛅ ☁️ 🌦️ 🌧️ ❄️ | SA | SU |

APPOINTMENTS

07:00 AM

08:00 AM

09:00 AM

10:00 AM

11:00 AM

12:00 PM

01:00 PM

02:00 PM

03:00 PM

04:00 PM

05:00 PM

06:00 PM

07:00 PM

08:00 PM

09:00 PM

NOTES

WATER INTAKE TOTAL:

DAILY PLANNER

DATE: | MO | TU | W
| TH | F
MOOD: 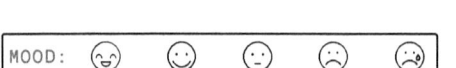 WEATHER: | SA | S

APPOINTMENTS

07:00 AM

08:00 AM

09:00 AM

10:00 AM

11:00 AM

12:00 PM

01:00 PM

02:00 PM

03:00 PM

04:00 PM

05:00 PM

06:00 PM

07:00 PM

08:00 PM

09:00 PM

NOTES

WATER INTAKE TOTAL:

DAILY PLANNER

DATE: [   ] MO TU WE
                    TH FR
MOOD: 😊 🙂 😐 🙁 😢   WEATHER:  SA SU

APPOINTMENTS

07:00 AM

08:00 AM

09:00 AM

10:00 AM

11:00 AM

12:00 PM

01:00 PM

02:00 PM

03:00 PM

04:00 PM

05:00 PM

06:00 PM

07:00 PM

08:00 PM

09:00 PM

NOTES

WATER INTAKE TOTAL:

🥛 🥛 🥛 🥛 🥛 🥛 🥛 🥛 🥛 🥛

DAILY PLANNER

MOOD: ☺ ☺ ☺ ☹ ☹

WEATHER:

APPOINTMENTS	NOTES
07:00 AM	
08:00 AM	
09:00 AM	
10:00 AM	
11:00 AM	
12:00 PM	
01:00 PM	
02:00 PM	
03:00 PM	
04:00 PM	
05:00 PM	
06:00 PM	
07:00 PM	
08:00 PM	
09:00 PM	

WATER INTAKE TOTAL:

DAILY PLANNER

DATE: ⬚ | MO | TU | WE |
| TH | FR |
MOOD: 😊 🙂 😐 🙁 ☹️   WEATHER: ☀️ ⛅ ☁️ 🌦️ 🌧️ ❄️ | SA | SU |

APPOINTMENTS

07:00 AM

08:00 AM

09:00 AM

10:00 AM

11:00 AM

12:00 PM

01:00 PM

02:00 PM

03:00 PM

04:00 PM

05:00 PM

06:00 PM

07:00 PM

08:00 PM

09:00 PM

NOTES

WATER INTAKE TOTAL:

95

DAILY PLANNER

DATE:

MO TU W

TH F

MOOD: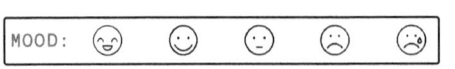

WEATHER: ☀ ⛅ ☁ 🌬 🌧 ❄

SA S

APPOINTMENTS	NOTES
07:00 AM	
08:00 AM	
09:00 AM	
10:00 AM	
11:00 AM	
12:00 PM	
01:00 PM	
02:00 PM	
03:00 PM	
04:00 PM	
05:00 PM	
06:00 PM	
07:00 PM	
08:00 PM	
09:00 PM	

WATER INTAKE TOTAL:

DAILY PLANNER

DATE:

MO	TU	WE
TH	FR
SA	SU

MOOD: 😊 ☺ 😐 ☹ 😞

WEATHER:

APPOINTMENTS

07:00 AM

08:00 AM

09:00 AM

10:00 AM

11:00 AM

12:00 PM

01:00 PM

02:00 PM

03:00 PM

04:00 PM

05:00 PM

06:00 PM

07:00 PM

08:00 PM

09:00 PM

NOTES

WATER INTAKE TOTAL:

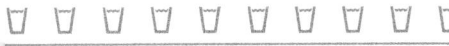

DAILY PLANNER

DATE: | MO | TU | W
TH | F
MOOD: 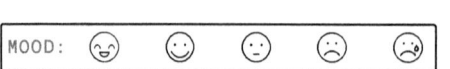 | WEATHER: | SA | S

APPOINTMENTS

| 07:00 AM |
| 08:00 AM |
| 09:00 AM |
| 10:00 AM |
| 11:00 AM |
| 12:00 PM |
| 01:00 PM |
| 02:00 PM |
| 03:00 PM |
| 04:00 PM |
| 05:00 PM |
| 06:00 PM |
| 07:00 PM |
| 08:00 PM |
| 09:00 PM |

NOTES

WATER INTAKE TOTAL:

96

DAILY PLANNER

DATE: | MO | TU | WE
TH | FR
SA | SU

MOOD: 😊 🙂 😐 ☹️ 😞

WEATHER: ☀️ ⛅ ☁️ 🌧️ ❄️

APPOINTMENTS	NOTES
07:00 AM	
08:00 AM	
09:00 AM	
10:00 AM	
11:00 AM	
12:00 PM	
01:00 PM	
02:00 PM	
03:00 PM	
04:00 PM	
05:00 PM	
06:00 PM	
07:00 PM	
08:00 PM	
09:00 PM	

WATER INTAKE TOTAL:
🥛 🥛 🥛 🥛 🥛 🥛 🥛 🥛 🥛 🥛

DAILY PLANNER

MOOD: 😊 🙂 😐 🙁 ☹️

WEATHER: ☀️ 🌤️ ☁️ 🌥️ 🌧️ ❄️

APPOINTMENTS

07:00 AM

08:00 AM

09:00 AM

10:00 AM

11:00 AM

12:00 PM

01:00 PM

02:00 PM

03:00 PM

04:00 PM

05:00 PM

06:00 PM

07:00 PM

08:00 PM

09:00 PM

NOTES

WATER INTAKE TOTAL:

DAILY PLANNER

DATE:

MO | TU | WE
TH | FR
SA | SU

MOOD: 😊 🙂 😐 🙁 ☹️

WEATHER:

APPOINTMENTS

07:00 AM

08:00 AM

09:00 AM

10:00 AM

11:00 AM

12:00 PM

01:00 PM

02:00 PM

03:00 PM

04:00 PM

05:00 PM

06:00 PM

07:00 PM

08:00 PM

09:00 PM

NOTES

WATER INTAKE TOTAL:

🥛 🥛 🥛 🥛 🥛 🥛 🥛 🥛 🥛 🥛

95

DAILY PLANNER

DATE:

MO TU W
TH F
SA S

MOOD: 😊 ☺ 😐 ☹ 😞

WEATHER: ☀ 🌤 ☁ 🌬 🌧 ❄

APPOINTMENTS

07:00 AM

08:00 AM

09:00 AM

10:00 AM

11:00 AM

12:00 PM

01:00 PM

02:00 PM

03:00 PM

04:00 PM

05:00 PM

06:00 PM

07:00 PM

08:00 PM

09:00 PM

NOTES

WATER INTAKE TOTAL:

DAILY PLANNER

DATE: | MO | TU | WE
TH | FR
MOOD: 😄 🙂 😐 🙁 😢   WEATHER: ☀ ⛅ ☁ 🌤 🌧 ❄ | SA | SU

APPOINTMENTS

07:00 AM

08:00 AM

09:00 AM

10:00 AM

11:00 AM

12:00 PM

01:00 PM

02:00 PM

03:00 PM

04:00 PM

05:00 PM

06:00 PM

07:00 PM

08:00 PM

09:00 PM

NOTES

WATER INTAKE TOTAL:
🥛 🥛 🥛 🥛 🥛 🥛 🥛 🥛 🥛 🥛

Re-Order

WWW.THE JOURNALBOX.COM
sales@thejournalbox.com | 215-298-9475
The Journal Box is a Woman, Minority & Veteran Owned Company
@2021 - The Journal Box